# BEGINNING
# Piano Solos

## 132 ORIGINAL MASTERPIECES
### Compiled and Edited by Paul Sheftel

D1710146

*N. Shoemaker #314 255-3785 Joyce*

## CARL FISCHER®
65 Bleecker Street, New York, NY 10012

ATF101

ISBN 0-8258-0343-8

5-18-153

# Table of Contents

# Preface

For any one who likes as I do to play "desert island" games — what books, music, records, toys, food, etc. would you want with you if you were stranded on a desert island? — compiling an anthology is a most challenging and yet appealing task. It was indeed in the "desert island" spirit that I set about assembling this collection, asking myself which piano pieces would I choose were I only to include my all time favorites, either from my experience as a student or as a teacher.

But why, some may ask, another anthology with many of the very familiar pieces which are already included elsewhere? To this I can only answer: because these are the classic pieces which are the heritage of every piano student. No compilation which purports to present a cross-section of piano literature could fail to include them.

My first consideration, then, was to try to include the most interesting and appealing examples from the "student literature" for while these books should be welcomed by all lovers of piano music they are primarily intended for the piano student.

Editing has deliberately been done with a light touch. In the cases of the Baroque and Classical examples for which there are few or no original indications, some musical suggestions have been provided; sparingly in some instances, in others, not at all. Edited examples are meant to serve as guidelines for those which are unedited, where students and teachers can exercise their own judgement regarding such matters as tempo, touch and dynamics. I have used Urtext sources whenever possible.

Fingerings have also been provided as sparingly as possible, in most instances only to indicate a change of position. Passages which recur are not fingered, thus obliging the student to recognize the return of a previously given passage, and to finger it accordingly. Fingering is, of course, very personal and students and teachers are always urged to explore alternative fingering possibilities.

The pieces within a given volume are, generally, at a comparable level of difficulty. *Beginning Piano Solos* presents the more elementary level, *More Classics • Romantics • Moderns* the most advanced, while *Classics • Romantics • Moderns* bridges the two levels. Grading, however, can be misleading since seemingly simple pieces can often present obstacles for some students, while so-called advanced pieces often prove to be surprisingly manageable. These classifications, therefore, should only be taken as very general guidelines.

It will be noted that certain composers are better represented than others. This apparent imbalance results from the obvious fact that some composers have been more prolific than others in writing inspired short piano pieces of only moderate difficulty.

In closing, the editor hopes that the many hours spent with these books may be rewarding ones to each of you and that if you should ever get to a "desert island" you may well remember to bring this repertoire with you.

P.S.

# Minuet

slow down

**JEAN-BAPTISTE LULLY**
(1632-1687)

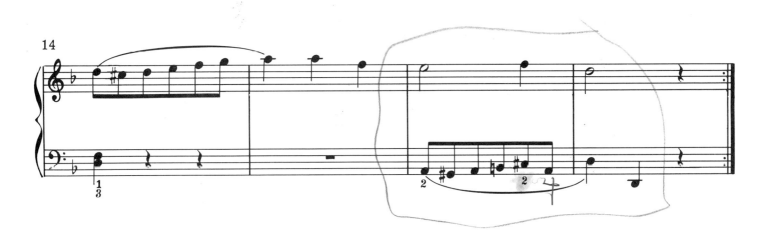

# Minuet

HENRY PURCELL
(1659-1695)

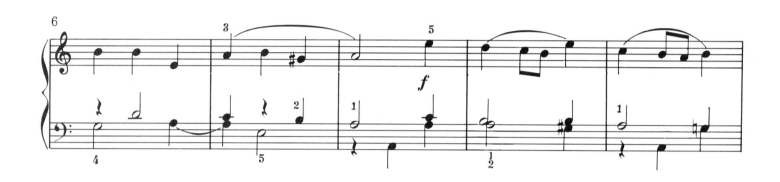

# Air

HENRY PURCELL
(1659-1695)

ATF101

# Le Petit Rien

(The Little Nothing)

FRANÇOIS COUPERIN
(1668-1708)

# Les Moissonneurs
## (The Reapers)

FRANÇOIS COUPERIN
(1668-1708)

# March

JEREMIAH CLARKE
*(ca.* 1673-1707)

ATF101

# Minuet

GEORG PHILIPP TELEMANN
(1681-1767)

# Passepied

GEORG PHILIPP TELEMANN
(1681-1767)

# Gigue

**GEORG PHILIPP TELEMANN**
(1681-1767)

ATF101

# Les Fifres
## (The Fifers)

JEAN FRANÇOIS DANDRIEU
(1682-1738)

# Minuet

JEAN-PHILLIPPE RAMEAU
(1683-1764)

# Le Lardon

## (The Joke)

**JEAN-PHILLIPPE RAMEAU**
(1683-1764)

# Polonaise

from the *Notebook for Anna Magdalena Bach*

JOHANN SEBASTIAN BACH, BWV Anh.119
(1685-1750)

# Musette

from the *Notebook for Anna Magdalena Bach*

JOHANN SEBASTIAN BACH, BWV Anh.126
(1685-1750)

# March

from the *Notebook for Anna Magdalena Bach*

**JOHANN SEBASTIAN BACH, BWV Anh.122**
(1685-1750)

# Minuet
from the *Notebook for Anna Magdalena Bach*

**JOHANN SEBASTIAN BACH, BWV Anh.114**
(1685-1750)

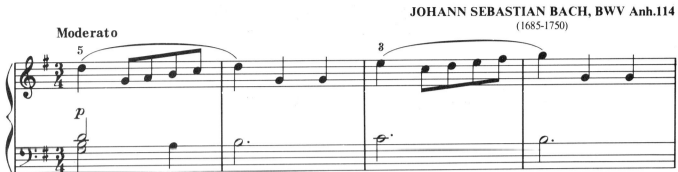

ATF101

# Minuet

from the *Notebook for Anna Magdalena Bach*

**JOHANN SEBASTIAN BACH, BWV Anh.116**
(1685-1750)

# Minuet

from the *Notebook for Anna Magdalena Bach*

**JOHANN SEBASTIAN BACH, BWV Anh.115**
(1685-1750)

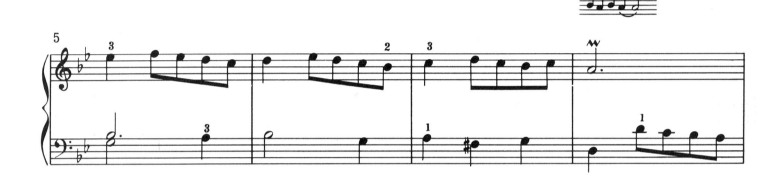

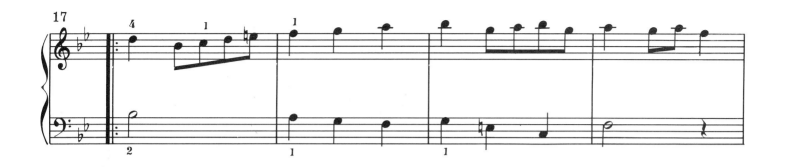

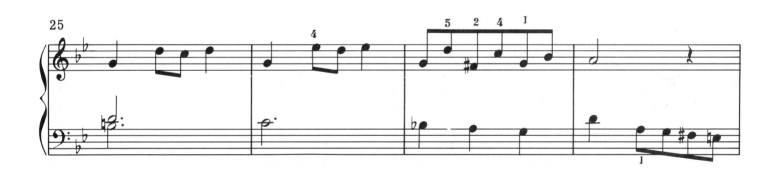

ATF101

# Minuet
from the *Notebook for Anna Magdalena Bach*

**JOHANN SEBASTIAN BACH, BWV Anh.132**
(1685-1750)

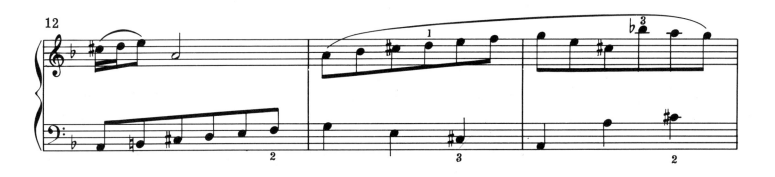

# Musette

"Gavotte II" from *English Suite No. 3*

JOHANN SEBASTIAN BACH, BWV 808
(1685-1750)

# Minuet

**JOHANN SEBASTIAN BACH**
(1685-1750)

# Minuet

from *French Suite No. 6*

**JOHANN SEBASTIAN BACH, BWV 817**
(1685-1750)

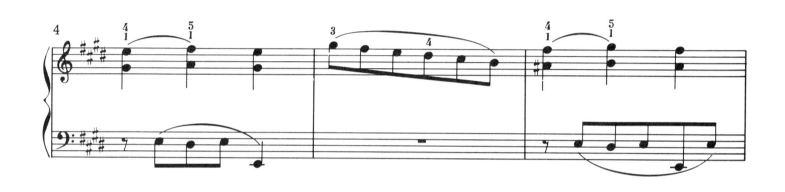

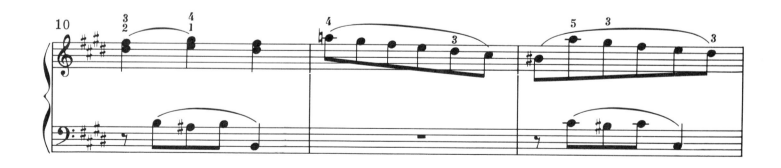

# Minuet

WILHELM FRIEDEMANN BACH
(1710-1784)

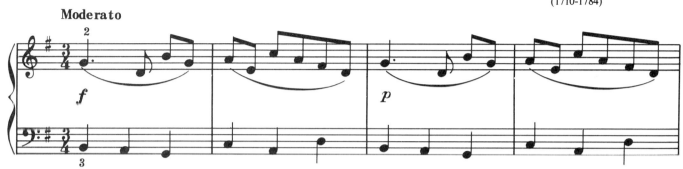

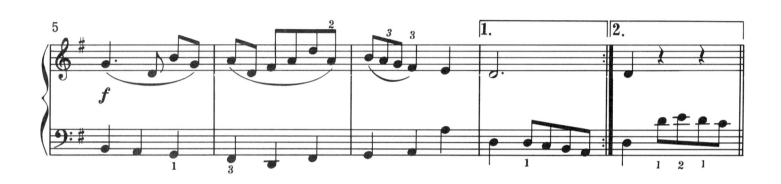

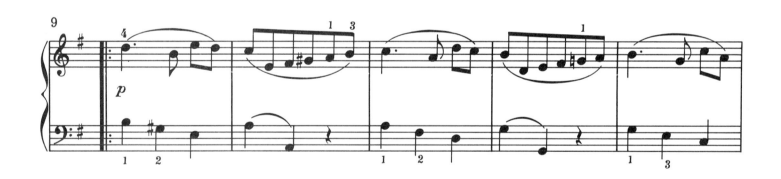

# Bourlesq

from *Notebook for Wolfgang*

**LEOPOLD MOZART**
(1719-1787)

ATF101

# Minuet

from *Notebook for Wolfgang*

LEOPOLD MOZART
(1719-1787)

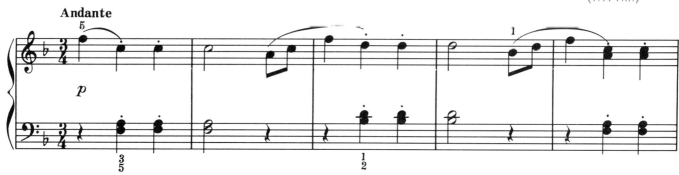

# Minuet

from *Notebook for Wolfgang*

LEOPOLD MOZART
(1719-1787)

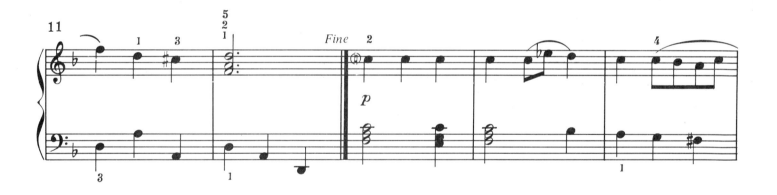

ATF101

# Bourrée

from *Notebook for Wolfgang*

**LEOPOLD MOZART**
(1719-1787)

# Minuet

from *Notebook for Nannerl*

LEOPOLD MOZART
(1719-1787)

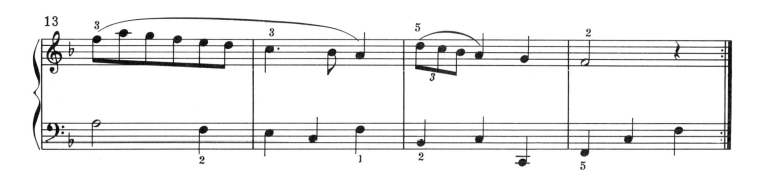

# Minuet

from *Notebook for Nannerl*

LEOPOLD MOZART
(1719-1787)

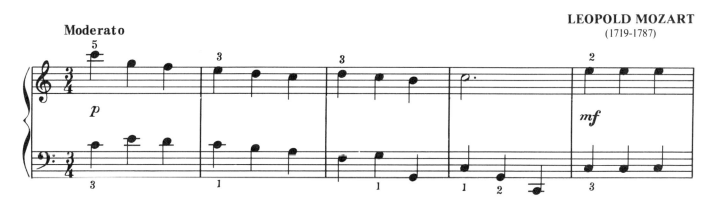

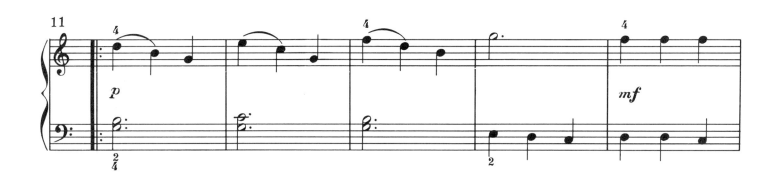

# Schwäbisch

JOHANN CHRISTOPH FRIEDRICH BACH
(1732-1795)

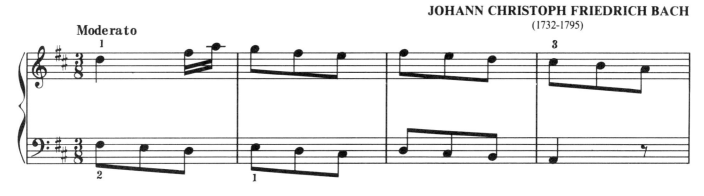

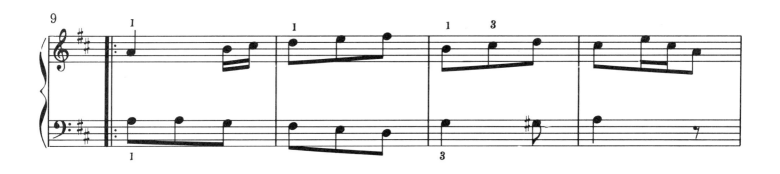

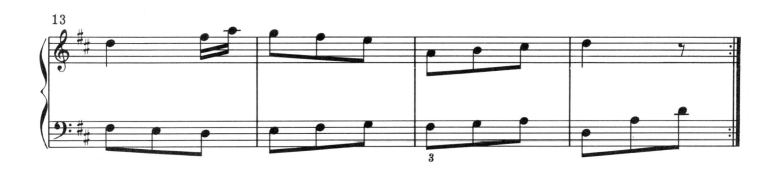

ATF101

# German Dance
## in E major

**FRANZ JOSEPH HAYDN**
(1732-1809)

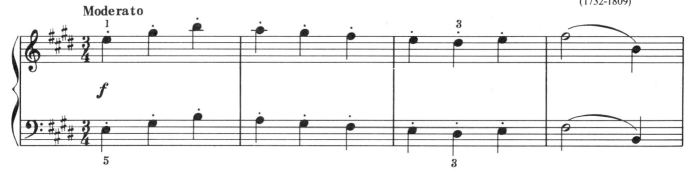

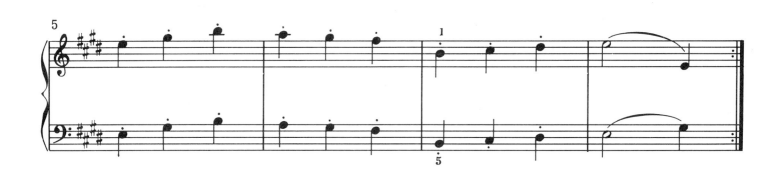

ATF101

# German Dance

in D major (no.1)

FRANZ JOSEPH HAYDN
(1732-1809)

Allegretto

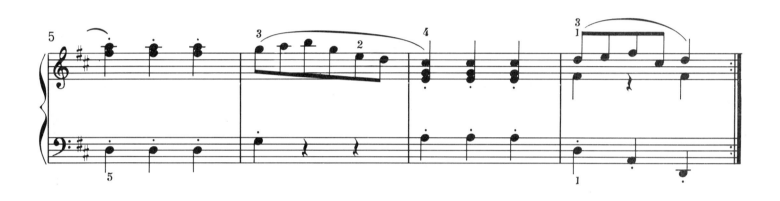

ATF101

# German Dance
in D major (no.2)

FRANZ JOSEPH HAYDN
(1732-1809)

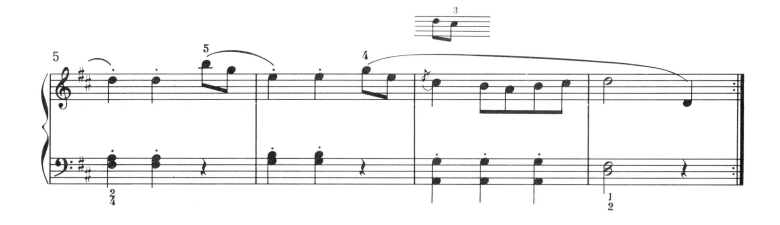

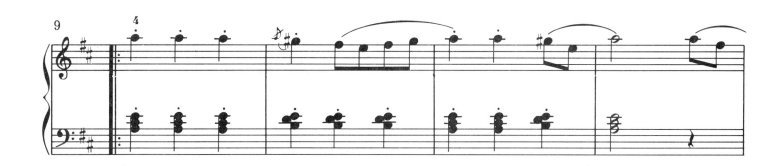

# German Dance

## in D major (no.3)

FRANZ JOSEPH HAYDN
(1732-1809)

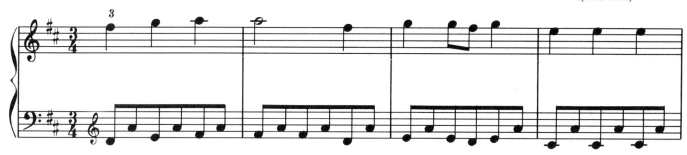

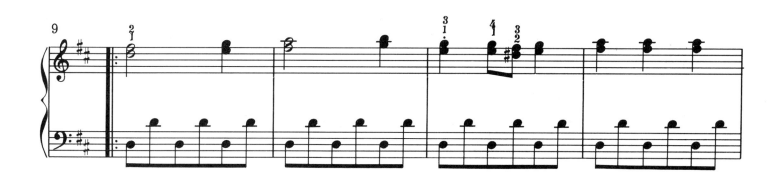

ATF101

# German Dance

in A major

FRANZ JOSEPH HAYDN
(1732-1809)

**Moderato**

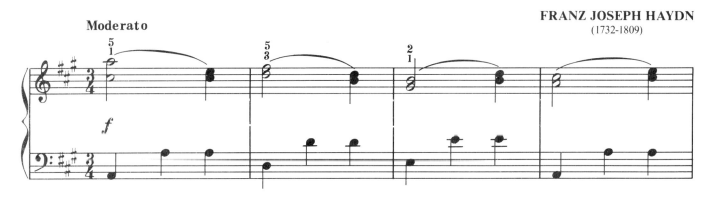

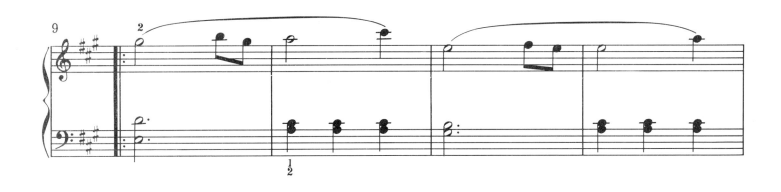

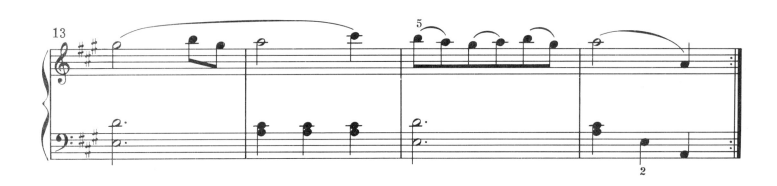

# German Dance
## in C major

FRANZ JOSEPH HAYDN
(1732-1809)

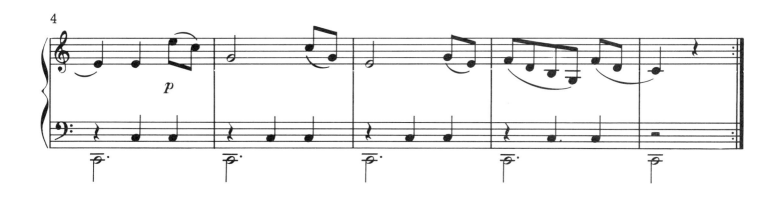

ATF101

# Minuet
## in G major

FRANZ JOSEPH HAYDN
(1732-1809)

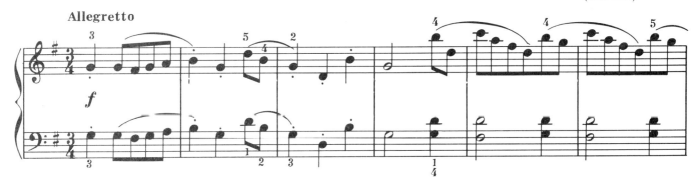

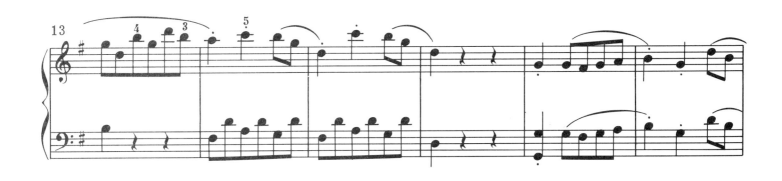

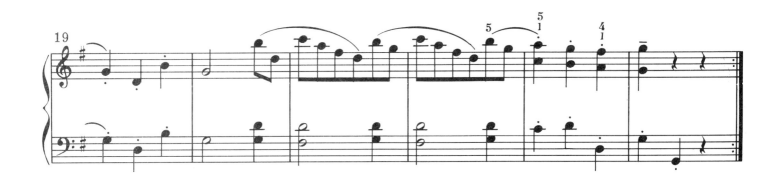

# Minuet
in A major

FRANZ JOSEPH HAYDN
(1732-1809)

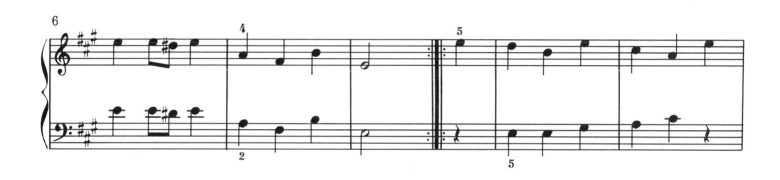

# Minuet

in D major

FRANZ JOSEPH HAYDN
(1732-1809)

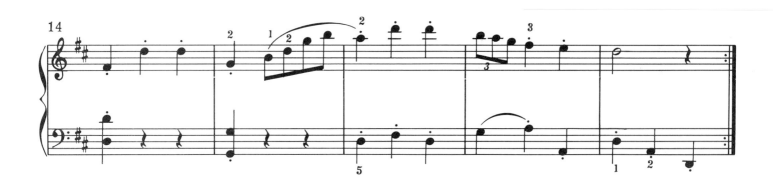

# Gypsy Dance

FRANZ JOSEPH HAYDN
(1732-1809)

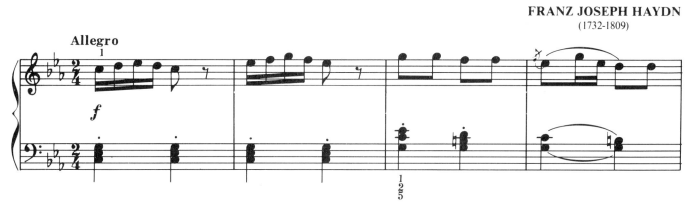

ATF101

Copyright © 1984 by Carl Fischer, Inc.

# Quadrille

FRANZ JOSEPH HAYDN
(1732-1809)

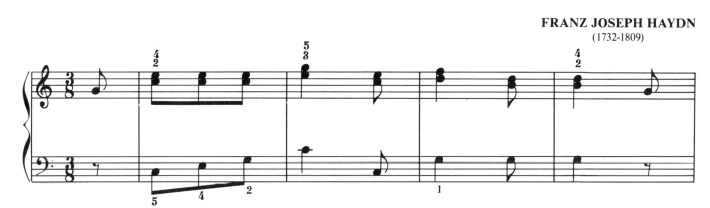

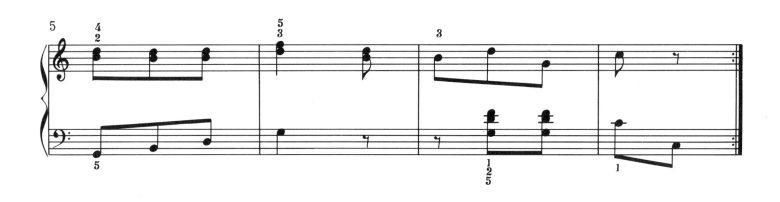

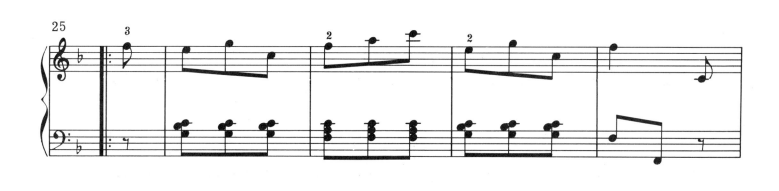

# Allemande

FRANZ JOSEPH HAYDN
(1732-1809)

# Fanfare

WILLIAM DUNCOMBE
(17??-17??)

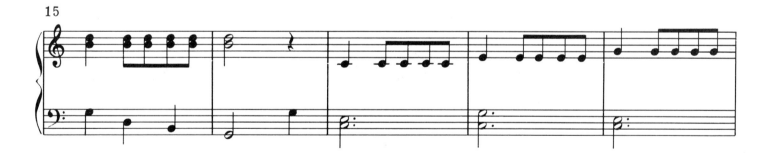

ATF101

# Gigue

WILLIAM DUNCOMBE
(17??-17??)

# Sonatina

**WILLIAM DUNCOMBE**
(17??-17??)

Moderato

ATF101

# Dance
from the *Guida di Musica* Collection

JAMES HOOK
(1746-1827)

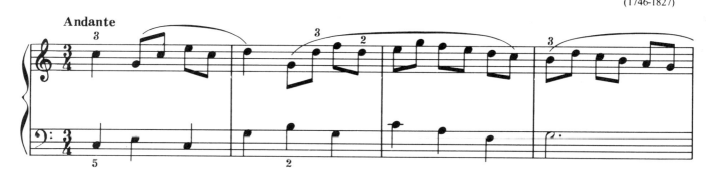

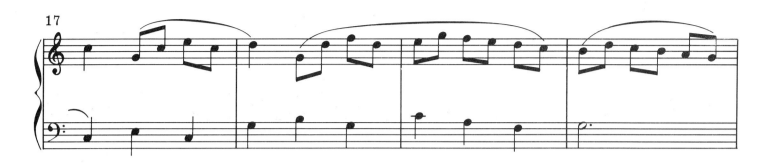

# Carefree

**DANIEL GOTTLOB TÜRK**
(1756-1813)

# Rondino

**DANIEL GOTTLOB TÜRK**
(1756-1813)

# The Dancing Master

DANIEL GOTTLOB TÜRK
(1756-1813)

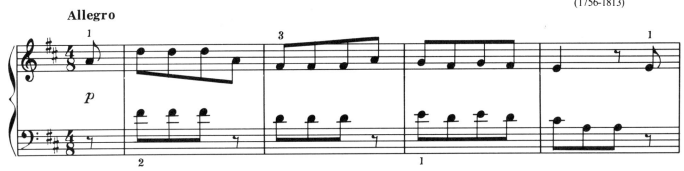

ATF101

# Hunting Horns with Echo

DANIEL GOTTLOB TÜRK
(1756-1813)

ATF101

# To the Little Finger of the Right Hand

DANIEL GOTTLOB TÜRK
(1756-1813)

# Arioso

**DANIEL GOTTLOB TÜRK**
(1756-1813)

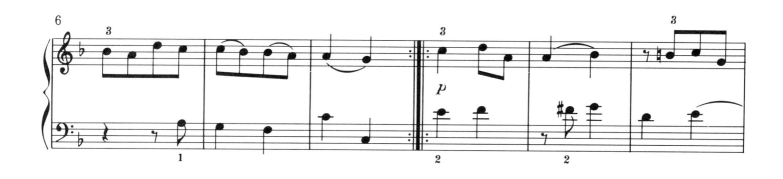

# Minuet

DANIEL GOTTLOB TÜRK
(1756-1813)

# Minuet and Trio

WOLFGANG AMADEUS MOZART, K.1
(1756 1791)

Allegretto

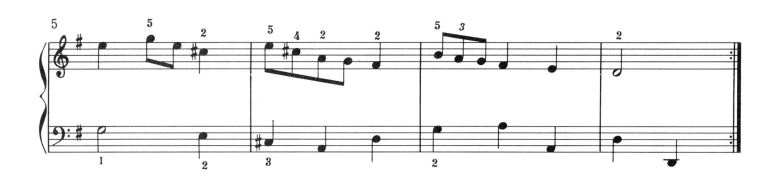

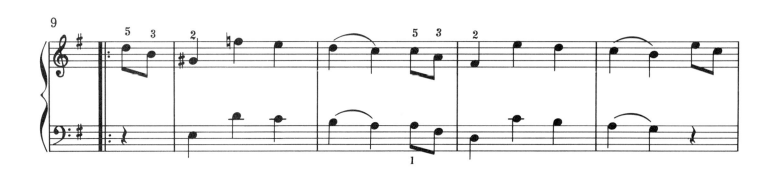

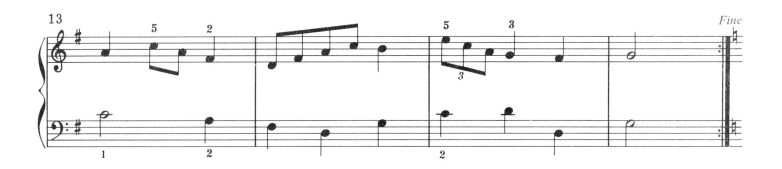

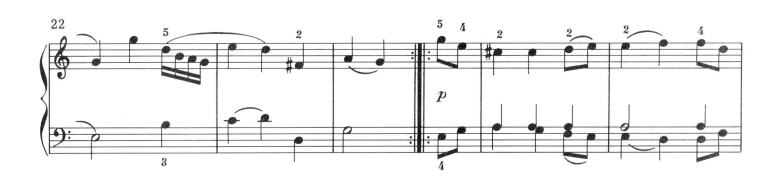

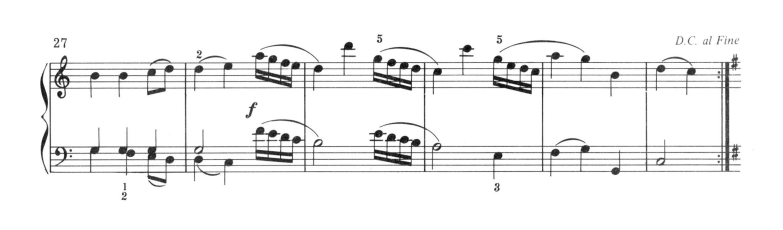

# Minuet

WOLFGANG AMADEUS MOZART, K.15
(1756-1791)

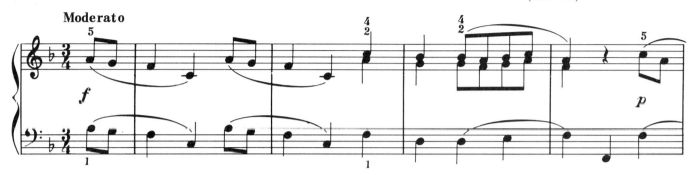

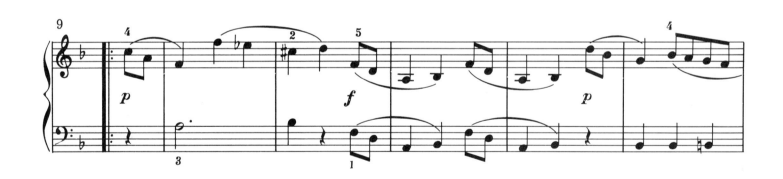

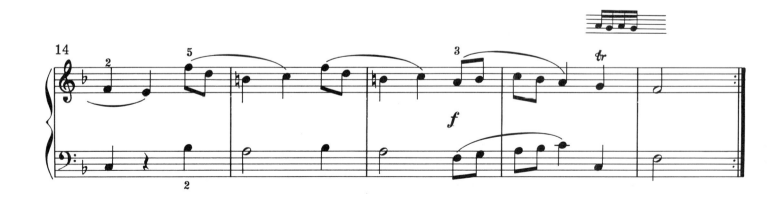

# Minuet

## (Menuetto I)

**WOLFGANG AMADEUS MOZART, K.6**
(1756-1791)

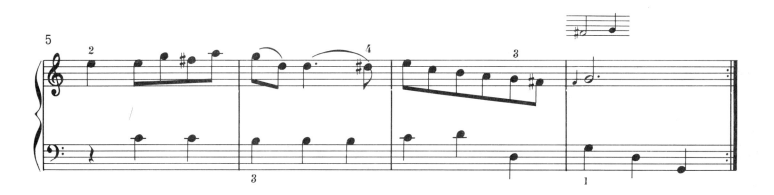

ATF101

# Minuet and Trio

WOLFGANG AMADEUS MOZART
(1756-1791)

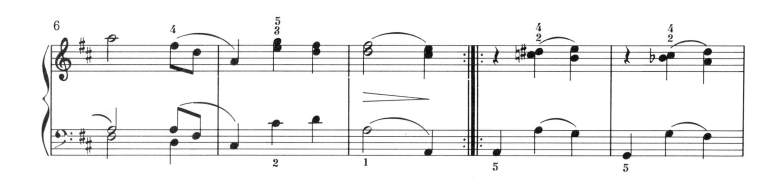

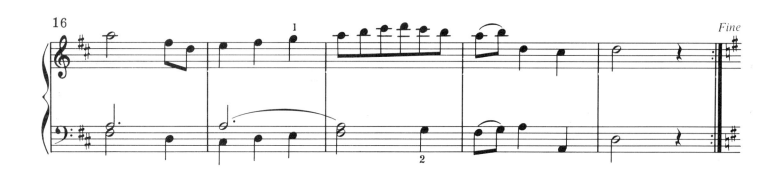

ATF101

**Trio**

*Da Capo al Fine*

# Minuet
## (Menuetto II)

WOLFGANG AMADEUS MOZART, K.6
(1756-1791)

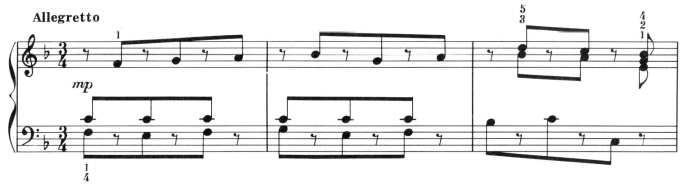

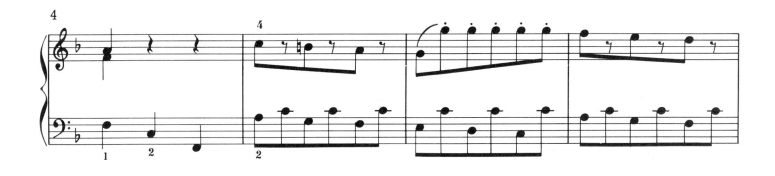

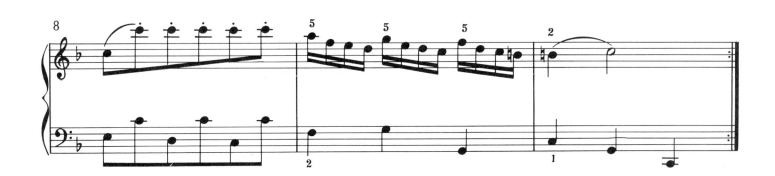

ATF101

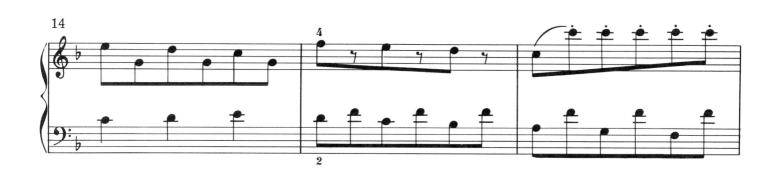

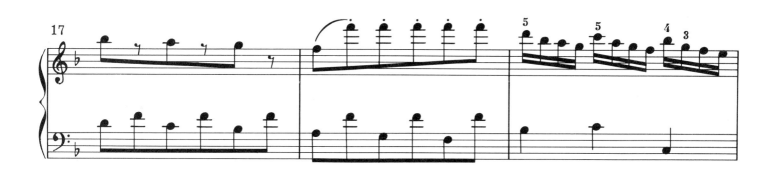

# Minuet

**WOLFGANG AMADEUS MOZART, K.5**
(1756-1791)

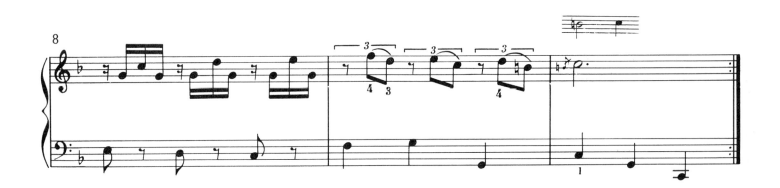

# Minuet

**WOLFGANG AMADEUS MOZART**
(1756-1791)

Allegretto

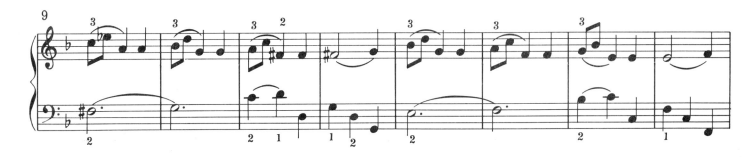

# German Dance

**WOLFGANG AMADEUS MOZART, K.605, No. 3**
(1756-1791)

Allegro

4TF101

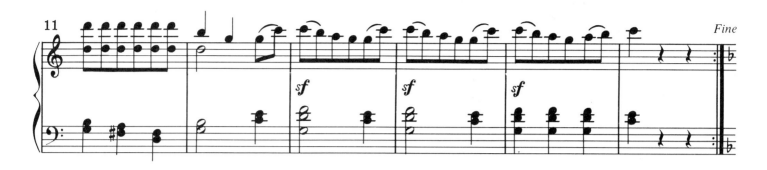

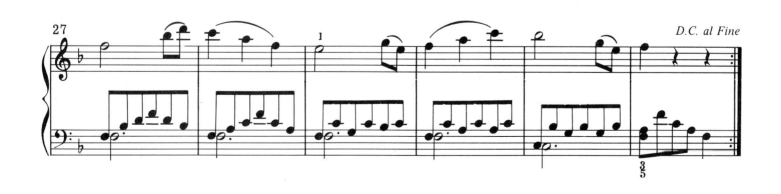

ATF101

# Air

**WOLFGANG AMADEUS MOZART**
(1756-1791)

# Allegro

**WOLFGANG AMADEUS MOZART, K.3**
(1756-1791)

# Andantino

WOLFGANG AMADEUS MOZART, KV.236(588b)
(1756-1791)

Copyright © 1984 by Carl Fischer, Inc.

# Russian Folk Song

**LUDWIG van BEETHOVEN, Op. 107, No. 7**
(1770-1827)

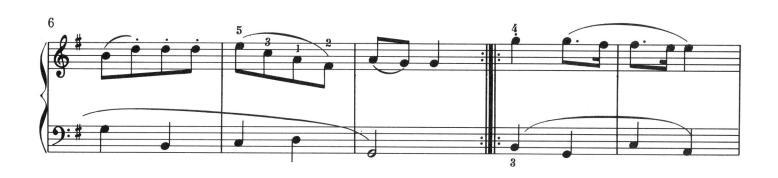

# Ecossaise
## in E♭ major

**LUDWIG van BEETHOVEN**
(1770-1827)

# Ecossaise
in G major

**LUDWIG van BEETHOVEN**
(1770-1827)

Copyright © 1984 by Carl Fischer, Inc.

# Russian Folk Song

in A minor

LUDWIG van BEETHOVEN
(1770-1827)

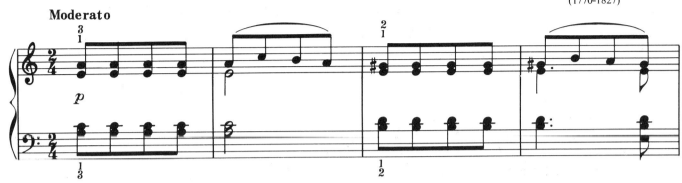

# Country Dance
## in D major (no.1)

LUDWIG van BEETHOVEN
(1770-1827)

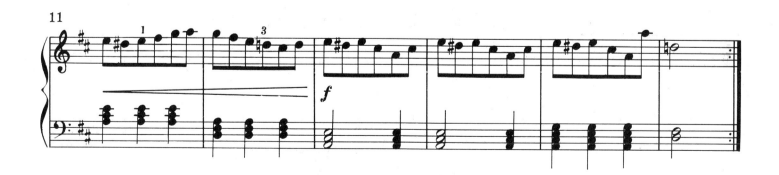

# Country Dance
## in D minor

LUDWIG van BEETHOVEN
(1770-1827)

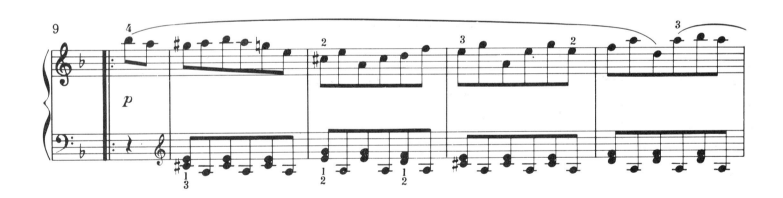

# Country Dance

in D major (no.2)

LUDWIG van BEETHOVEN
(1770-1827)

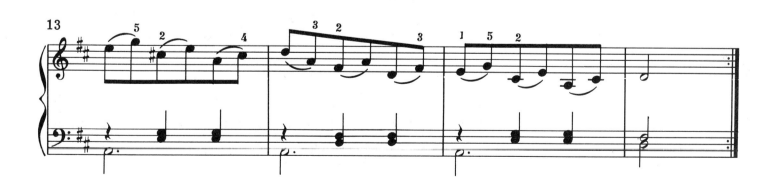

ATF101

# German Dance

in C major

LUDWIG van BEETHOVEN
(1770-1827)

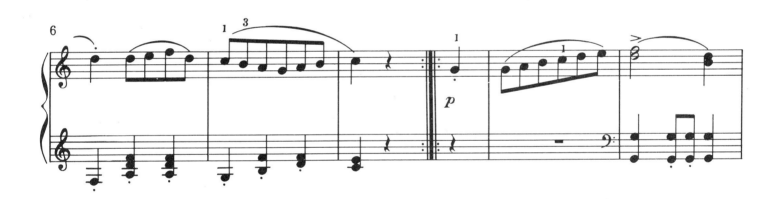

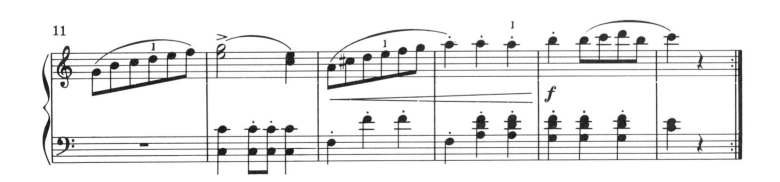

# German Dance

### in A major

LUDWIG van BEETHOVEN
(1770-1827)

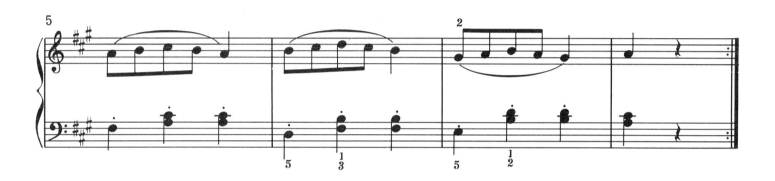

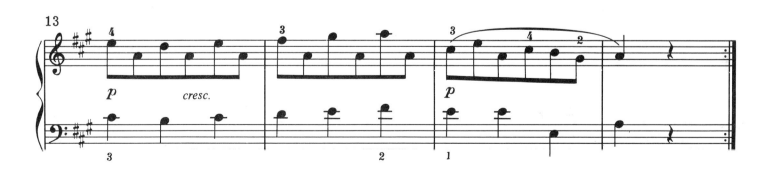

ATF101

# German Dance
### in G major (no.1)

**LUDWIG van BEETHOVEN**
(1770-1827)

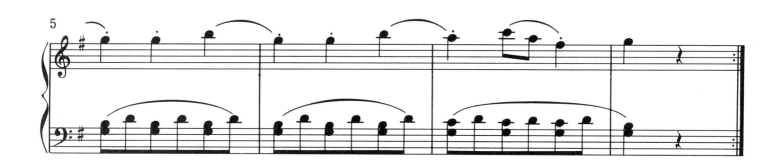

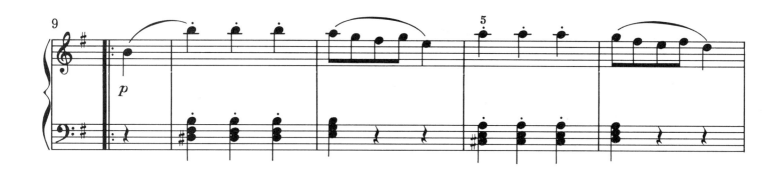

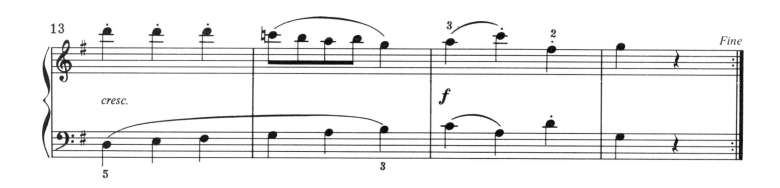

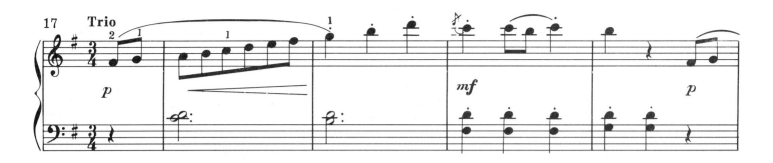

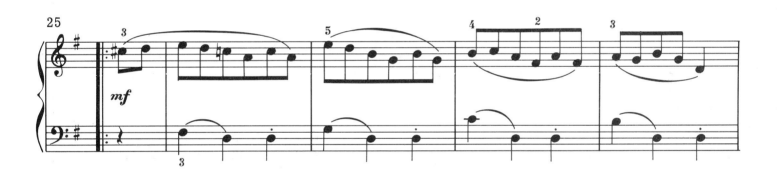

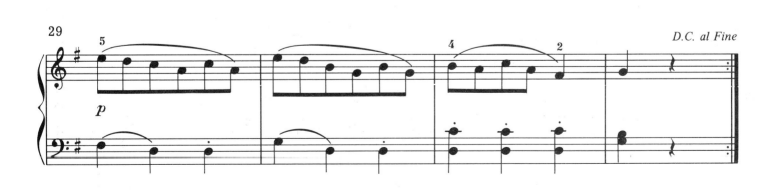

ATF101

# German Dance
in G major (no.2)

LUDWIG van BEETHOVEN
(1770-1827)

# German Dance
in D major (no.1)

LUDWIG van BEETHOVEN
(1770-1827)

# German Dance

in E♭ major

**LUDWIG van BEETHOVEN**
(1770-1827)

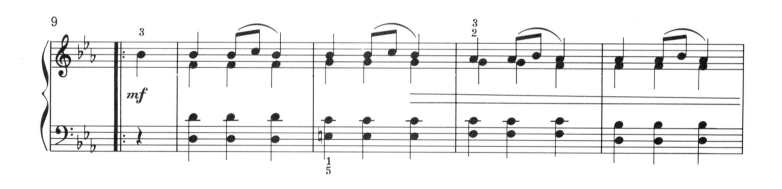

Da Capo al Fine

# German Dance

in D major (no.2)

**LUDWIG van BEETHOVEN**
(1770-1827)

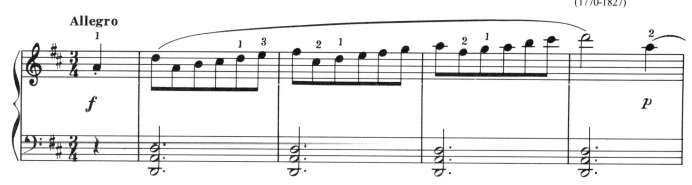

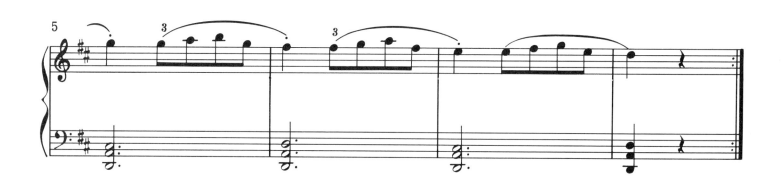

# German Dance
in F major

LUDWIG van BEETHOVEN
(1770-1827)

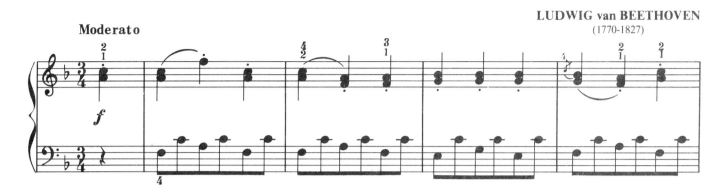

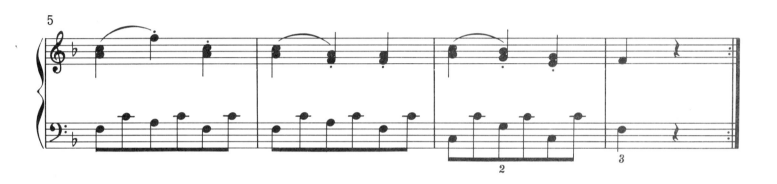

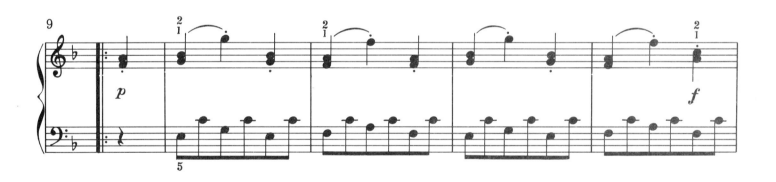

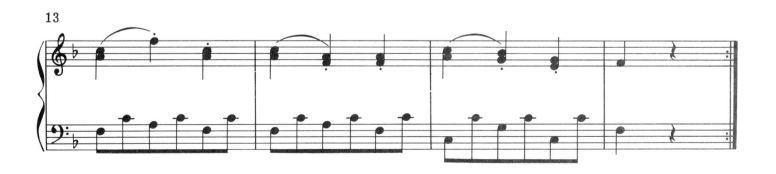

ATF101

# Bagatelle
## in G major

ANTON DIABELLI
(1781-1858)

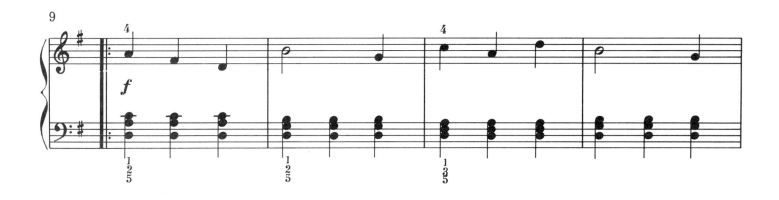

ATF101

# Bagatelle
## in C major

ANTON DIABELLI
(1781-1858)

# Six Etudes

CARL CZERNY
(1791-1857)

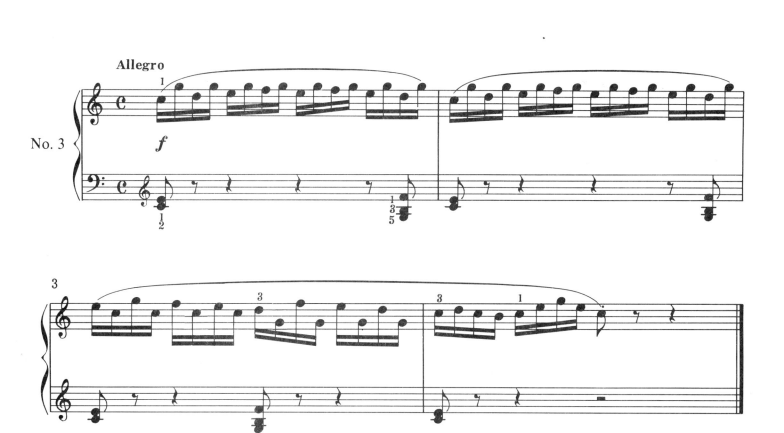

No. 5

No. 6

# Polka

MICHAEL IVANOVICH GLINKA
(1804-1857)

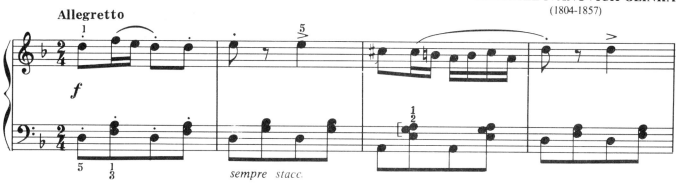

# L'Arabesque

**JOHANN FRIEDRICH BURGMÜLLER**
(1806-1874)

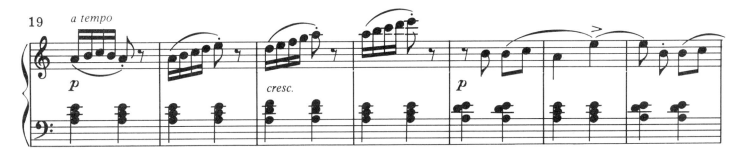

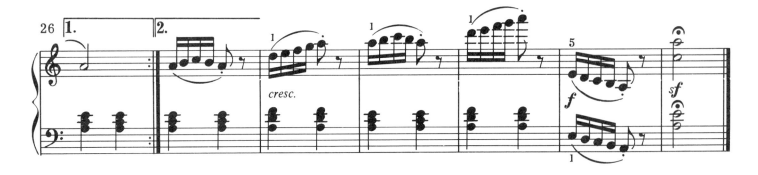

# Innocence

JOHANN FRIEDRICH BURGMÜLLER
(1806-1874)

# Restlessness

JOHANN FRIEDRICH BURGMÜLLER
(1806-1874)

Allegro agitato

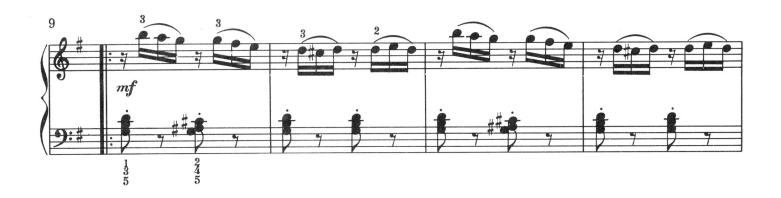

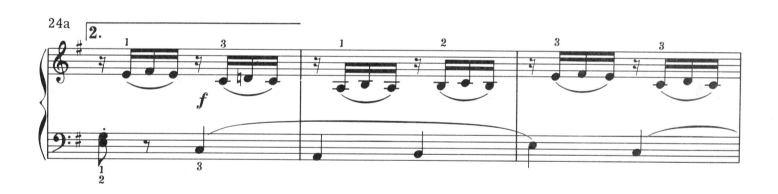

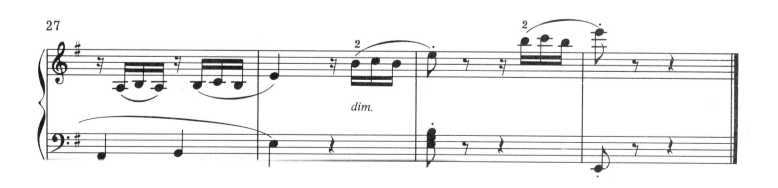

# Progress

JOHANN FRIEDRICH BURGMÜLLER
(1806-1874)

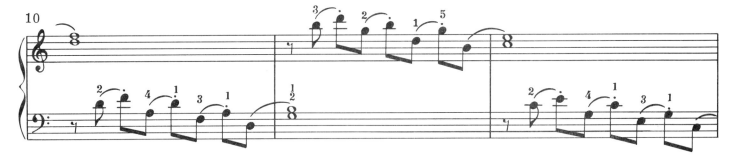

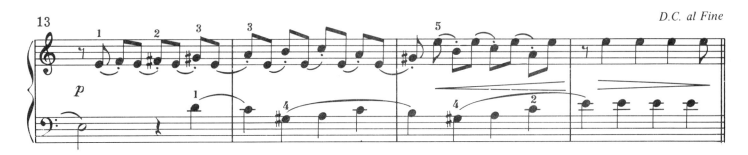

Copyright © 1984 by Carl Fischer, Inc.

# The Limpid Stream

**JOHANN FRIEDRICH BURGMÜLLER**
(1806-1874)

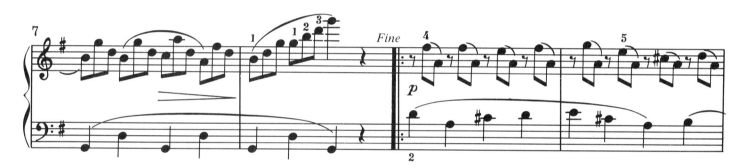

# Melody

(Melodie)

from *Album for the Young*

ROBERT SCHUMANN, Op. 68, No. 1
(1810-1856)

*The fingering in italics is by Schumann.

ATF101

# Soldier's March

(Soldatenmarsch)

from *Album for the Young*

ROBERT SCHUMANN, Op. 68, No. 2
(1810-1856)

Tempo di marcia
(Munter und straff)

Copyright © 1984 by Carl Fischer, Inc.

# Little Piece
### (Stückchen)
from *Album for the Young*

ROBERT SCHUMANN, Op. 68, No. 5
(1810-1856)

# Poor Orphan

(Armes Waisenkind)

from *Album for the Young*

ROBERT SCHUMANN, Op. 68, No. 6
(1810-1856)

Copyright © 1984 by Carl Fischer, Inc.

# Wild Horseman
## (Wilder Reiter)
### from *Album for the Young*

**ROBERT SCHUMANN, Op. 68, No. 8**

# First Loss

(Erster Verlust)

from *Album for the Young*

ROBERT SCHUMANN, Op. 68, No. 16
(1810-1856)

# Musette

FELIX LE COUPPEY
(1811-1887)

# The Sick Doll

from *Album for the Young*

PETER ILYICH TCHAIKOVSKY, Op. 39, No. 6
(1840-1893)

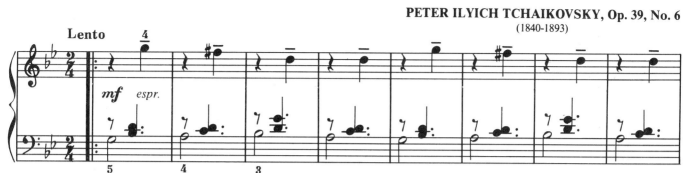

ATF101

# The Bear

VLADIMIR REBIKOFF
(1866-1920)

# Playing Soldiers

VLADIMIR REBIKOFF, Op. 31, No. 4
(1866-1920)

# Dialogue

No. 3 from *First Term at the Piano*

BÉLA BARTÓK
(1881-1945)

# Dialogue

No. 5 from *First Term at the Piano*

BÉLA BARTÓK
(1881-1945)

# Dance

No. 6 from *First Term at the Piano*

BÉLA BARTÓK
(1881-1945)

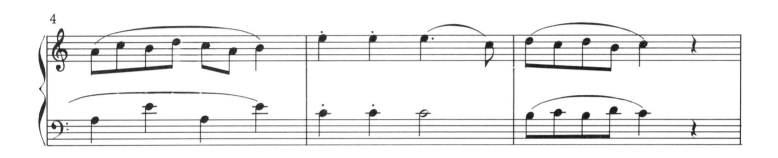

ATF101

# Folk Dance

No. 8 from *First Term at the Piano*

BÉLA BARTÓK
(1881-1945)

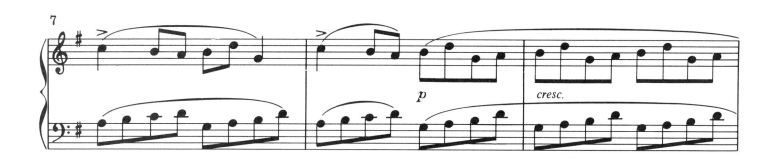

# Folk Song

No. 10 from *First Term at the Piano*

BÉLA BARTÓK
(1881-1945)

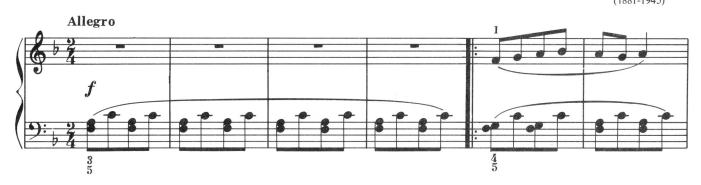

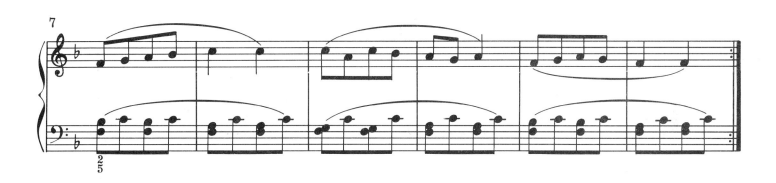

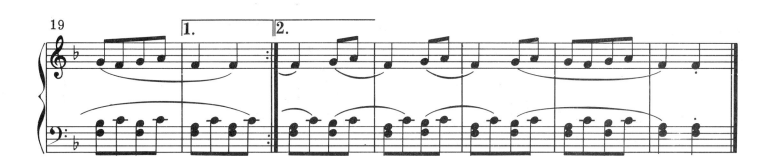

ATF101

# Minuet

No. 11 from *First Term at the Piano*

BÉLA BARTÓK
(1881-1945)

# Children at Play

No. 1 from *For Children*, Vol. 1

BÉLA BARTÓK
(1881-1945)

# Song

No. 3 from *For Children*, Vol. 1

BÉLA BARTÓK
(1881-1945)

# Children's Dance

No. 10 from *For Children*, Vol. 1

BÉLA BARTÓK
(1881-1945)

# Play

No. 5 from *For Children*, Vol. 1

BÉLA BARTÓK
(1881-1945)

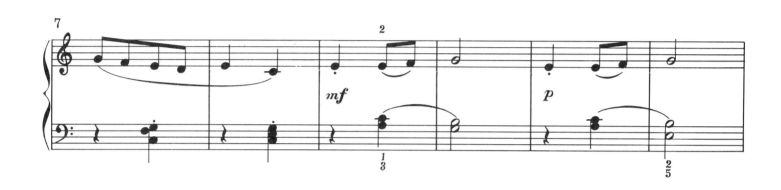

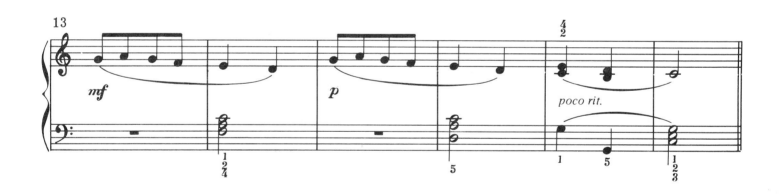

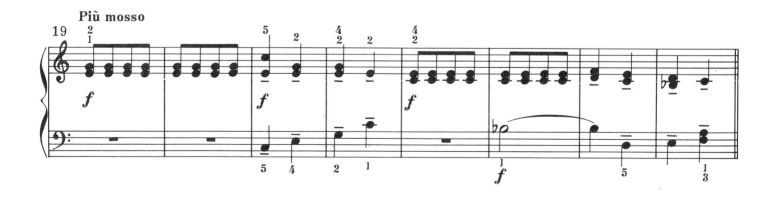

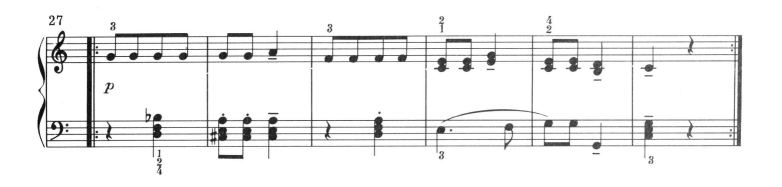

# Study for the Left Hand

No. 6 from *For Children*, Vol. 1

BÉLA BARTÓK
(1881-1945)

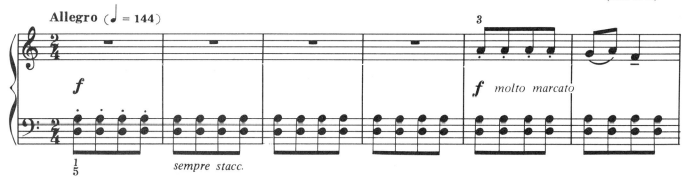

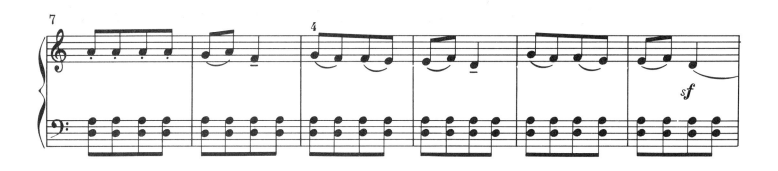

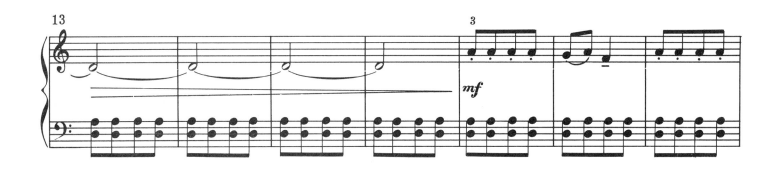

# Springtime Song

No. 2 from *For Children, Vol. 1*

BÉLA BARTÓK
(1881-1945)

136

# Touches Noires
## (Black Keys)

**DARIUS MILHAUD**
(1892-1974)

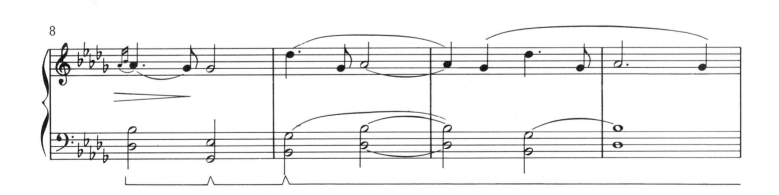

# Touches Blanches

## (White Keys)

DARIUS MILHAUD
(1892-1974)

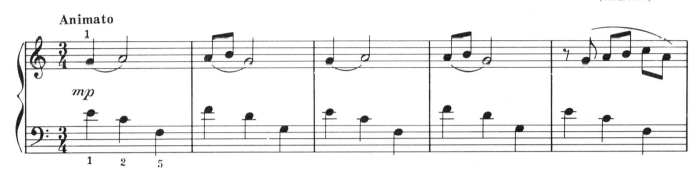

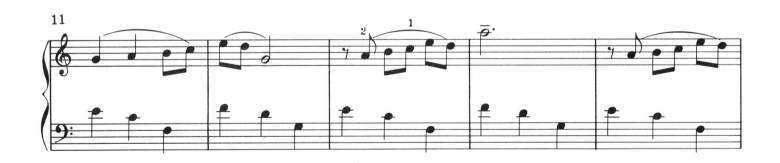

ATF101

# Careful Etta

from *Tintypes*

DOUGLAS MOORE
(1893-1969)

141

ATF101

# Enchantment

HOWARD HANSON
(1896-1981)

# Melody

from *24 Pieces for Children*

**DMITRI KABALEVSKY, Op. 39, No. 1**
(1904-1987)

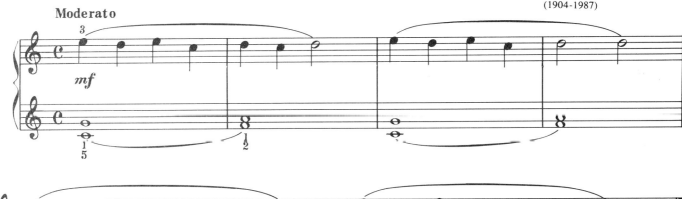

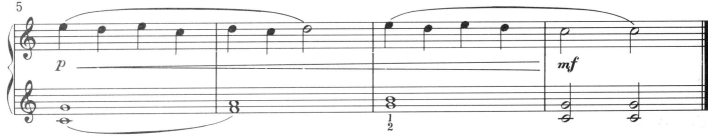

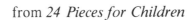

# A Little Joke

from *24 Pieces for Children*

**DMITRI KABALEVSKY, Op. 39, No. 6**
(1904-1987)

# Funny Event

from *24 Pieces for Children*

DMITRI KABALEVSKY, Op. 39, No. 7
(1904-1987)

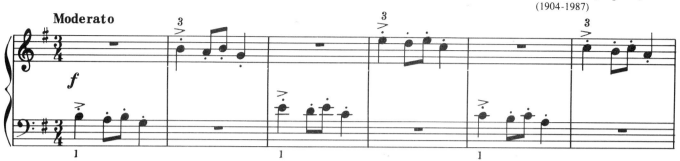

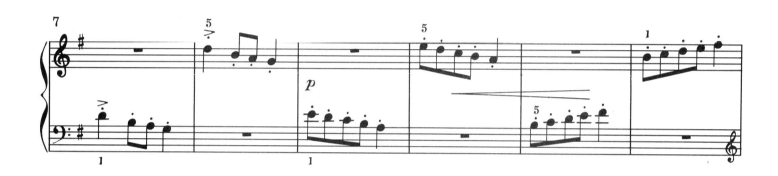

# Song

from *24 Pieces for Children*

DMITRI KABALEVSKY, Op. 39, No. 8
(1904-1987)

# Dance

from *24 Pieces for Children*

DMITRI KABALEVSKY, Op. 39, No. 9
(1904-1987)

# March

from *24 Pieces for Children*

**DMITRI KABALEVSKY, Op. 39, No. 10**
(1904-1987)

Energico

Copyright © 1984 by Carl Fischer, Inc.

# Scherzo

from *24 Pieces for Children*

DMITRI KABALEVSKY, Op. 39, No. 12
(1904-1987)

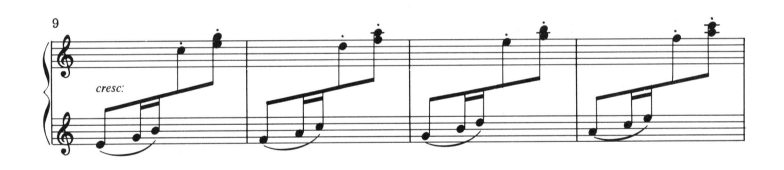

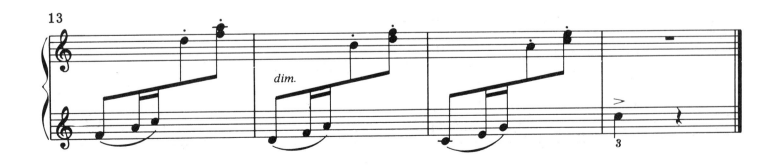

ATF101

# A Fable

from *24 Pieces for Children*

**DMITRI KABALEVSKY, Op. 39, No. 14**
(1904-1987)

**Allegro moderato**

ATF101

# Jumping

from *24 Pieces for Children*

**DMITRI KABALEVSKY**, Op. 39, No. 15
(1904-1987)

# Little Song

from *30 Pieces for Children*

**DMITRI KABALEVSKY, Op. 27, No. 2**
(1904-1987)

# Playing Ball

from *30 Pieces for Children*

DMITRI KABALEVSKY, Op. 27, No. 5
(1904-1987)

Copyright © 1984 by Carl Fischer, Inc.

# Clowning

from *30 Pieces for Children*

**DMITRI KABALEVSKY, Op. 27, No. 10**
(1904-1987)

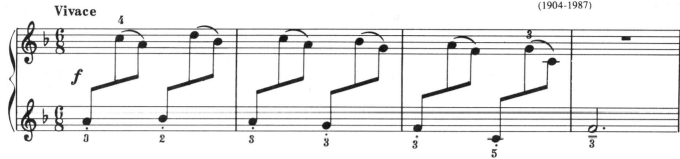

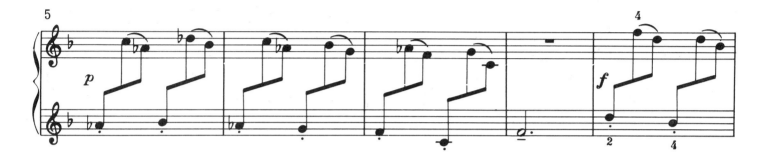

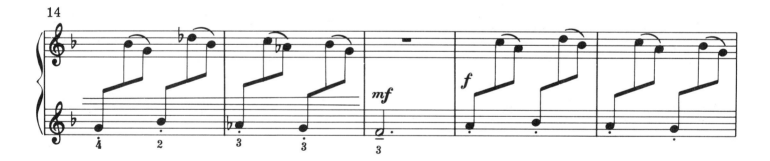

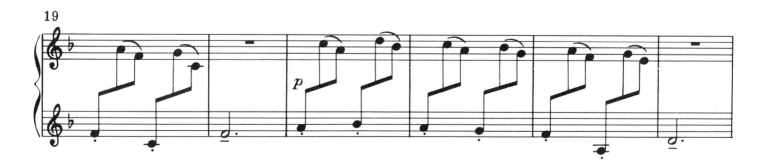

ATF101

# Little Fable

from *30 Pieces for Children*

DMITRI KABALEVSKY, Op. 27, No. 9
(1904-1987)

# Waltz

from *24 Pieces for Children*

DMITRI KABALEVSKY, Op. 39, No. 13
(1904-1987)

ATF101

# *About Paul Sheftel...*

    Paul Sheftel is a nationally recognized leader in the area of keyboard studies. His published materials are widely used throughout the country. In his role as educator, he has performed, lectured and conducted workshops in virtually every state in the U.S. He has been a pioneer in the creation and development of instructional materials utilizing MIDI technology. His software is in use nationwide as well as in many countries throughout Europe and Asia. He has composed electronic orchestrations to Carl Fischer's "Music Pathways" piano course as well as for other collections in the Fischer catalog.

    In addition to his private teaching studio in New York City, Paul Sheftel heads the undergraduate piano pedagogy program at the Manhattan School of Music, and is piano editor for Carl Fischer. He is also cofounder and director of Sound Start Electronic Publications, developers of MIDI-enhanced software.